DENVER
BRONCOS

by Brian Howell

Published by ABDO Publishing Company, 8000 West 78th Street, Edina, Minnesota 55439. Copyright © 2011 by Abdo Consulting Group, Inc. International copyrights reserved in all countries. No part of this book may be reproduced in any form without written permission from the publisher. SportsZone™ is a trademark and logo of ABDO Publishing Company.

Printed in the United States of America,
North Mankato, Minnesota
062010
092010

Editor: Matt Tustison
Copy Editor: Nicholas Cafarelli
Interior Design and Production: Christa Schneider
Cover Design: Christa Schneider

Photo Credits: Paul Jasienski/AP Images, cover; Paul Sakuma/AP Images, title page, 31; Cliff Grassmick/AP Images, 4; Elise Amendola/AP Images, 7; Ed Reinke/AP Images, 8, 43 (middle); David Stluka/AP Images, 11, 34, 43 (bottom), 44; NFL Photos/AP Images, 12, 16, 18, 21; Jerry Mosey/AP Images, 15, 42 (top); AP Images, 22, 25, 33, 42 (middle, bottom); Ron Heflin/AP Images, 26, 43 (top); NFL Photos/AP Images, 29; Lenny Ignelzi/AP Images, 37; Chris Schneider/AP Images, 39; Mel Evans/AP Images, 40; Ed Andrieski/AP Images, 47

Library of Congress Cataloging-in-Publication Data
Howell, Brian, 1974-
  Denver Broncos / Brian Howell.
     p. cm. — (Inside the NFL)
  Includes index.
  ISBN 978-1-61714-010-5
  1. Denver Broncos (Football team)—History—Juvenile literature. I. Title.
  GV956.D4H69 2011
  796.332'640978883—dc22
                                        2010014962

TABLE OF CONTENTS

CHAPTER 1

REACHING THE TOP

During a career that lasted 16 seasons, John Elway was known for an ability to beat opponents with a powerful arm. Few quarterbacks in National Football League (NFL) history have thrown for as many yards and touchdowns as Elway did for the Denver Broncos.

Yet, the play for which Elway will best be remembered was not a pass. It was not even a touchdown. That defining moment took place during Super Bowl XXXII on January 25, 1998, at Qualcomm Stadium in San Diego, California.

RESPECT FOR THE AFC

Going into Super Bowl XXXII, the National Football Conference (NFC) had won 13 straight Super Bowls. The Broncos were responsible for three of those 13 losses for the American Football Conference (AFC). By beating the Packers, the Broncos broke the NFC's streak. Starting with Denver's win, the AFC won nine of the next 12 Super Bowls, including two in a row for the Broncos.

DENVER'S 31–24 WIN OVER GREEN BAY IN JANUARY 1998 GAVE QUARTERBACK JOHN ELWAY AND THE BRONCOS A LONG-AWAITED SUPER BOWL TRIUMPH.

PAIN AND GLORY

As much as John Elway meant to the Broncos, it was running back Terrell Davis who was named the Most Valuable Player (MVP) of Super Bowl XXXII. He ran 30 times for 157 yards and a Super Bowl-record three touchdowns—including a go-ahead 1-yard score with less than two minutes remaining in Denver's win over Green Bay.

The performance was even more remarkable considering Davis missed the entire second quarter. A migraine headache kept him out of the game.

Davis's story of success was surprising. The Broncos chose the former University of Georgia player in the sixth round of the 1995 NFL Draft. But he rushed for 1,117 yards as a rookie. He then ran for 1,538 yards in his second season, 1,750 in his third, and 2,008 in his fourth. Injuries hampered him the next three years. He retired before the 2002 season.

The Broncos found themselves in a 17–17 tie with the Green Bay Packers late in the third quarter.

On a crucial play, Elway dropped back to pass. He could not find a receiver, so he took off running to his right. With Packers defenders closing in, Elway put his head down and dove forward. The 37-year-old quarterback was hit and spun through the air. He dropped to the ground after an 8-yard gain.

The play set up a 1-yard touchdown run by Terrell Davis that gave Denver a 24–17 lead.

"That let you know what the game meant. That lets you know the magnitude of this

THE BRONCOS' JOHN ELWAY IS UPENDED ON A KEY FIRST-DOWN RUN IN SUPER BOWL XXXII. "HE INSPIRED US," TIGHT END SHANNON SHARPE SAID.

ballgame, what this game meant to him. When I saw that, I said, 'If he throws anything in my vicinity, I'm catching it. I'm not going to give any excuses. I'm going to get it.' He inspired us," tight end Shannon Sharpe said.

Denver went on to win the game 31–24, giving the Broncos the first Super Bowl championship in team history. Although the game was full of heroes, it was Elway's play that defined it.

Before the 1997 season, the Broncos had never prevailed in

> **"That let you know what the game meant. That lets you know the magnitude of this ballgame, what this game meant to him. When I saw that, I said, 'If he throws anything in my vicinity, I'm catching it.'"**
> —Shannon Sharpe, on John Elway's crucial run in Super Bowl XXXII

a Super Bowl. They had come close. They had been to football's biggest game four times—three with Elway as quarterback—and had lost all four times.

The 1997 Broncos would not be denied. It was fitting that Elway—who ranks among the NFL's all-time leaders in touchdown throws and passing yards—led them to the title.

THE HEAD MAN

Pat Bowlen purchased the Broncos in 1984. He helped them reach the Super Bowl five times through the 2009 season. The Wisconsin native had careers in oil, gas, and real estate before getting involved with the Broncos. In addition to owning the team, Bowlen stays physically active and has competed in the Ironman Triathlon.

DENVER'S TERRELL DAVIS CELEBRATES A TOUCHDOWN RUN IN SUPER BOWL XXXII. DAVIS RUSHED FOR 157 YARDS AND THREE TOUCHDOWNS.

After the game, the Broncos hoisted the Lombardi Trophy, given to the Super Bowl winner each year.

Team owner Pat Bowlen declared, "This one's for John!"

Winning the Super Bowl was the perfect cap to Elway's career. But he was not done.

Elway played one more season, and the Broncos performed even better than they had in 1997. Elway led the Broncos to a second straight Super Bowl title after the 1998 season. This time they beat the Atlanta Falcons 34–19 at Pro Player Stadium in Miami, Florida. Elway was selected as the game's MVP.

It took the Broncos 38 seasons to win a Super Bowl. Then they became just the seventh team to win two in a row.

As for Elway, before Super Bowl XXXII he was known as a great player who could not win the big game. Then he ended his career with back-to-back Super Bowl titles.

As of 2010, he was the only starting quarterback in NFL history whose last game was a Super Bowl victory.

SUPER TRIPS

Through the 2009 season, the Broncos had played in six Super Bowls. Only two teams had played in more. They were the Dallas Cowboys (eight) and Pittsburgh Steelers (seven). The New England Patriots had also been to six Super Bowls.

JOHN ELWAY HOLDS THE SUPER BOWL TROPHY DENVER WON FOR BEATING ATLANTA 34–19. ELWAY ENDED HIS CAREER WITH BACK-TO-BACK NFL TITLES.

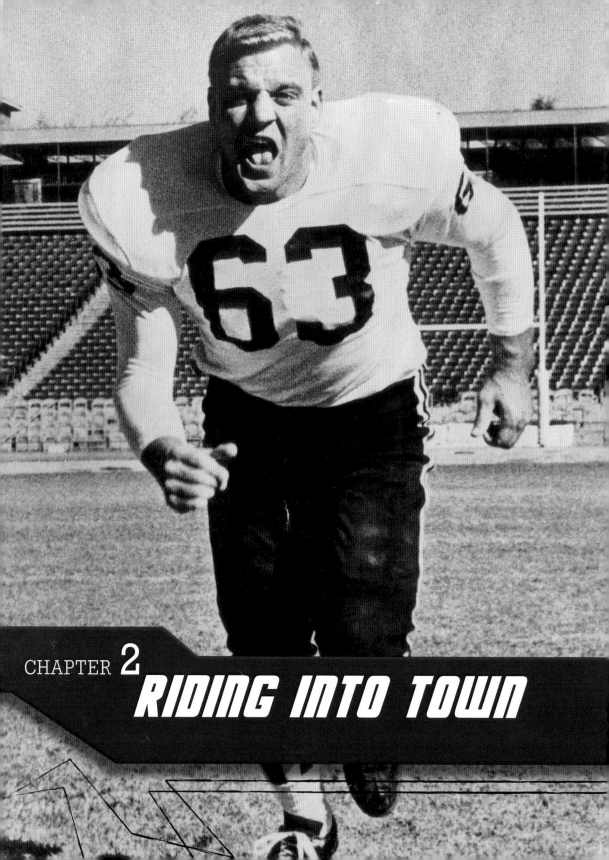

CHAPTER 2

RIDING INTO TOWN

Today, Denver has a lively professional sports scene. It is one of a few U.S. cities with pro teams in the NFL (Broncos), the National Basketball Association (Denver Nuggets), the National Hockey League (Colorado Avalanche), and Major League Baseball (Colorado Rockies).

That was not always the case, however. Before 1960, the city's only professional team was the Denver Bears, a minor league baseball team. At the time, pro football was gaining in popularity. Two Texas oilmen—Lamar Hunt and Bud Adams—saw an opportunity. Unable to buy NFL teams, Hunt and Adams made plans for the creation of the American Football League (AFL). Hunt and Adams sought

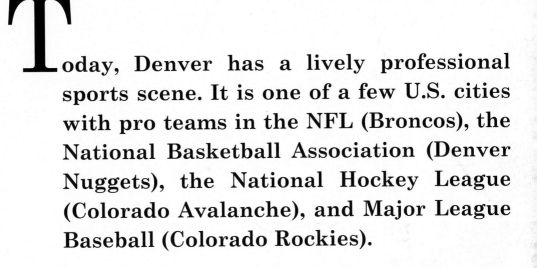

FASHION STATEMENT

When the Broncos were born in 1960, they wore brown and yellow uniforms with vertical striped socks. The Broncos wore those colors for just two years. Before the 1962 season, new coach Jack Faulkner held a ceremonial burning of the uniforms. At that point, the Broncos began wearing orange and blue—the colors they still wear.

OFFENSIVE LINEMAN BUZZ GUY PLAYED FOR DENVER IN 1961. THE BRONCOS WERE ONE OF THE AFL'S EIGHT ORIGINAL TEAMS IN 1960.

out business partners, including Denver Bears executives.

"It took us completely by surprise. We had talked about getting more use out of Bears Stadium, but nobody even mentioned football. It sounded crazy, but we went ahead anyway," said Gerald H. Phipps, who was on the Bears' board of directors.

When the AFL began play in 1960, there were eight teams, including the Denver Broncos. On September 9, 1960, the Broncos made history by playing in the AFL's first game. They beat the host Boston Patriots 13–10. Four games into their first season, the Broncos were 3–1. Tough times were ahead, though.

The Broncos ended the 1960 season 4–9–1. Their record would not improve much throughout

DYNAMIC DUO

The Broncos did not win many games during the 1960s. Still, quarterback Frank Tripucka and wide receiver Lionel Taylor were among the AFL's brightest stars. The two played together during the Broncos' first four seasons. Both were AFL all-stars in 1962. Taylor played seven seasons with the Broncos (1960–66) and led the league in receiving in five of its first six seasons. Tripucka was a Bronco for four seasons (1960–63) and was one of the AFL's best quarterbacks during that time.

their first decade of existence. The first five years were especially tough, on and off the field. The Broncos were losing, and their long-term future in Denver was in doubt.

The Broncos faced several disadvantages. They were underpaid, they played in a baseball stadium, and their brown and yellow uniforms were ugly. They were laughed at by their

BRONCOS QUARTERBACK FRANK TRIPUCKA DRIVES THROUGH THE NEW YORK TITANS' LINE FOR A TOUCHDOWN ON SEPTEMBER 30, 1962, IN NEW YORK.

GERALD H. PHIPPS, *ABOVE*, AND HIS BROTHER ALLAN PURCHASED THE BRONCOS IN 1965 AND PROMISED TO KEEP THEM IN DENVER.

opponents. The fans did not jump on board, either. Through the Broncos' first two seasons, they averaged fewer than 12,000 fans per game at Bears Stadium.

Before the 1962 season and again before the 1965 season, there were rumors of the Broncos leaving Denver. Brothers Gerald

SAVING THE TEAM

Gerald H. Phipps served on the board of directors for the Rocky Mountain Empire Sports, Inc., and owned a construction company that rebuilt Bears Stadium. By the end of 1964, the Broncos were in debt and their owners wanted to sell the team. The Broncos nearly left Denver. However, on February 15, 1965, Phipps and his brother Allan purchased the team and promised to keep it in Denver. In 1981, they sold it to Edgar Kaiser, who then sold it to Pat Bowlen in 1984.

and Allan Phipps would not let that happen, however. Once they purchased the team in 1965, they turned the Broncos around. "Nothing would hurt us more than headlines around the country saying Denver had lost its football team," Gerald Phipps said.

The Broncos did not leave. In fact, there was more support for the team than ever before. The Broncos sold 8,000 season tickets in 1964 and nearly 23,000 in 1965. Finally, the Broncos had a solid future in Denver. It would be a long time before they would start winning, though. In 10 seasons during the 1960s, the Broncos never had a winning record and never made the playoffs.

THE FIRST SUPERSTAR

Despite their poor record in the 1960s, the Broncos had some great players during the decade. Running back Floyd Little was among them.

Denver selected Little in the first round, sixth overall, in the 1967 AFL/NFL combined draft. He had been a standout at Syracuse University, following in the footsteps of previous Orangemen star running backs Jim Brown and Ernie Davis.

Little played nine seasons in Denver and ran for 6,323 yards. He retired as the Broncos' all-time leading rusher. In 1971, Little ran for 1,133 yards to lead the NFL and become the first Bronco to rush for 1,000 yards in a season.

In 1984, he was inducted into the Broncos' Ring of Fame, the team's Hall of Fame. In 2010, he was elected to the Pro Football Hall of Fame. Legendary Denver quarterback John Elway has referred to Little as "the greatest Bronco of them all."

CHAPTER 3
GROWING UP

Before the 1970 season, the 10 teams in the AFL merged with the 16 teams in the NFL to create a larger NFL. It was a new beginning for the Broncos. Losing seasons continued for another few years. That was about to change, however.

In 1972, the Broncos hired John Ralston as their coach. He had been a successful coach at Stanford University. Now his task was to turn the Broncos around. This would not be easy. But Ralston believed in the team. "We're going to win the Super Bowl," he said. The Broncos never did win a Super Bowl with Ralston, however. In fact, he never even took them to the playoffs. But he did turn the Broncos around.

During Ralston's five seasons (1972–76), he brought in

LINEMAN LYLE ALZADO WAS PART OF THE BRONCOS' "ORANGE CRUSH" DEFENSE THAT HELPED THE TEAM IMPROVE IN THE 1970s.

great talent and led the Broncos to their first winning season, in 1973. He also guided them to winning seasons in 1974 and 1976. The seventh coach in Broncos history, Ralston was the first one to finish with a winning record (34–33–3).

Despite Ralston's success, he did not lead the team to the postseason and the players did not want him as their coach anymore. He quit after the 1976 season.

The next coach of the Broncos was Robert "Red" Miller. His goal was to finally take the Broncos to the playoffs. "We had some very talented players. Overall, we had a squad that needed a player here or some improvement there to become a championship team," he said.

In trying to make the Broncos a championship team, Miller knew what the team's problem was. Up to that point in their history, the Broncos rarely had stability at quarterback. Miller was certain that had to change.

"I needed a veteran who had been there to get us there again," he said. One of his first moves as coach was to trade for Craig Morton, who had played 12 seasons in the NFL with the Dallas Cowboys and New York Giants.

ORANGE CRUSH

The Broncos had played well on defense even before Red Miller took over as coach. Known as the "Orange Crush," the Broncos' defense gave up very few points in 1976 and even fewer in 1977. Star players such as linemen Barney Chavous, Rubin Carter, and Lyle Alzado, linebackers Randy Gradishar and Tom Jackson, and defensive backs Louis Wright, Steve Foley, and Billy Thompson helped the defense excel.

LINEBACKER TOM JACKSON PLAYED HIS ENTIRE CAREER WITH DENVER, FROM 1973 TO 1986. HE LATER BECAME AN NFL BROADCASTER ON ESPN.

With Miller and Morton leading the way in 1977, the Broncos finally became a championship team. They won their first six games in 1977 and did not stop there. They finished the regular season with the best record (12–2) in team history to that point. The Broncos also won their first division championship and qualified for the playoffs for the first time. Their success captured the hearts of the fans in Denver, who had waited so long to experience a winning team.

The Broncos had the entire city behind them. They carried the momentum throughout the 1977 playoffs, defeating the Pittsburgh Steelers and Oakland Raiders in games at Mile High Stadium. (Bears Stadium had been upgraded and renamed in 1968.) That led to a date with the Cowboys in Super Bowl XII in New Orleans, Louisiana.

For the first time, the Broncos reached the biggest stage in professional football. Just before they ran out to the field, Broncos linebacker Tom Jackson and defensive back Billy Thompson stopped for a minute to take in what was happening. "We both looked out and it was a sea of orange. I said, 'Hey, man, we're here. We're gonna get this one,'" Thompson said.

KEYWORTH'S HIT

Broncomania was at an all-time high when Broncos fullback Jon Keyworth made headlines off the field. An accomplished musician, he wrote a song about the team titled, "Make Those Miracles Happen." Nearly 50,000 copies of the song sold in Denver during 1977. Keyworth was scheduled to sing the song on The Tonight Show—but only if the Broncos won the Super Bowl. They did not, so he never got the chance.

WIDE RECEIVER HAVEN MOSES CELEBRATES IN THE BRONCOS' 20–17 WIN OVER THE RAIDERS IN THE AFC CHAMPIONSHIP GAME ON JANUARY 1, 1978.

BRONCOMANIA

It took more than 10 years for the fans in Denver to fully embrace the Broncos. Once they did, the fans never wavered in their loyalty.

Except for two games during the 1987 players' strike, every home game from 1970 through 2009 was a sellout. There is no question it was the 1977 season, however, that brought Broncomania to a new level.

"There was more done that year to bring people together than I've ever seen in my life. It transformed the attitudes of this city," said Haven Moses, a Broncos wide receiver from 1972 to 1981.

In fact, one of the most recognizable figures in Broncos history was not a player but a fan. Tim McKernan became known as the Barrel Man. Beginning in 1977, he wore just a Broncos barrel, a cowboy hat, and boots to games—even on cold days. McKernan retired the barrel in 2007. He passed away in 2009.

Super Bowl XII did not go the way the Broncos had hoped, however. Morton threw four interceptions, and the Broncos committed eight total turnovers. The Cowboys controlled the game nearly all day. Dallas won 27–10. "We couldn't do anything right," Morton said.

Although the Broncos lost the Super Bowl, they were a different team from that point on. No longer a joke, the Broncos were the pride of Denver. They would become a team that got used to winning. Having never been to the playoffs before 1977, they went back in 1978 and 1979.

BRONCOS QUARTERBACK CRAIG MORTON REACTS AFTER THE COWBOYS' ED "TOO TALL" JONES TACKLED HIM IN SUPER BOWL XII. DALLAS WON 27–10.

CHAPTER 4
ELWAY'S TEAM

As exciting as Super Bowl XII was for the Broncos' fans in January 1978, that passion could not last forever. Big changes came to the team just a few years later.

The Broncos missed the playoffs in 1980. Shortly after that season, the Phipps brothers sold the team to Edgar Kaiser. Red Miller was fired by Kaiser, who hired young Dan Reeves to become the coach. Quarterback Craig Morton was nearing the end of his career, as were other key players from the 1977 squad. By the end of the 1982 season, the Broncos needed a new spark.

They needed a star. In the spring of 1983, the Broncos found that star.

Entering the 1983 NFL Draft, the Baltimore Colts had the No. 1 pick. They intended to use it to select a rocket-armed quarterback from Stanford University named John Elway. Elway, however, did not want to play for the Colts under their owner, Robert Irsay. Also a

QUARTERBACK JOHN ELWAY WAS A STAR IN THE 1980s. HE LED THE BRONCOS TO THE SUPER BOWL AFTER THE 1986, 1987, AND 1989 SEASONS.

talented baseball player, Elway had played in the minor leagues in the New York Yankees' farm system. He said he would consider playing baseball instead of football if Baltimore drafted him.

At the draft in April 1983, the Colts made Elway the No. 1 pick. Elway insisted that he would never play for the Colts. So, on May 2, 1983, Baltimore traded Elway to Denver for offensive tackle Chris Hinton, quarterback Mark Herrmann, a first-round pick in 1984, and $1 million. Denver had its star.

From the start, Elway was looked upon as the man who would turn the Broncos around. Every one of his moves was reported by the Denver media. Elway had no idea what he was

KARL MECKLENBURG

Making a trade for quarterback John Elway was Denver's key move in 1983. However, the Broncos picked up another player that spring who would go on to become one of the team's greats. Linebacker Karl Mecklenburg, from the University of Minnesota, was not selected by the Broncos until the twelfth round of the NFL Draft. He had to battle to even make the team in 1983. He went on to play 12 seasons with Denver and was selected to six Pro Bowls.

getting into. At the conclusion of his first news conference, Elway told a Broncos employee, "Well, I'm glad this press stuff is done with."

Elway did not know it at the time, but that was just the beginning for him. The media reported about what he wore, what he ate, where he went after practice. "The toughest thing about my rookie year was the media. They wore me out," Elway said.

LINEBACKER KARL MECKLENBURG, SHOWN IN 1992, WAS DENVER'S TWELFTH-ROUND DRAFT CHOICE IN 1983. HE BECAME A SURPRISE STANDOUT.

The pressure to turn the Broncos around wore him out too. Elway struggled through his rookie year, although he did help Denver get to the playoffs for the first time in four years. The Broncos lost 31–7 in the first round to the host Seattle Seahawks.

Although he had a difficult rookie season, Elway quickly proved to be the key player for whom the Broncos had been hoping. He got them to the Super Bowl after his fourth season, in 1986, and again after the 1987 and 1989 seasons.

WINNING WAYS

The Broncos qualified for the playoffs just three times during their first 23 seasons, from 1960 to 1982. They went 2–3 in their playoff games during that time. During John Elway's 16 seasons, the Broncos went to the playoffs 10 times and played in five Super Bowls, winning two of them. With Elway as quarterback, the Broncos were 14–8 in playoff games.

Elway did not just help the Broncos win games; he helped them win in dramatic fashion. Elway often displayed a knack for leading his team to improbable victories. That began with a come-from-behind win over, of all teams, the Colts during his rookie season. In fact, during his career, Elway led 47 game-saving or game-winning drives.

"I just liked the ball in my hands with a chance to win the game. All you wanted was a chance, and I was lucky to play with a lot of great players who helped make some of those comebacks possible," Elway said.

Elway and Reeves had their differences. But they learned to coexist and win together. Most important, Elway's teammates grew to appreciate the weapon

QUARTERBACK JOHN ELWAY AND COACH DAN REEVES DID NOT ALWAYS SEE EYE TO EYE, BUT THEY LED THE BRONCOS TO MANY WINS.

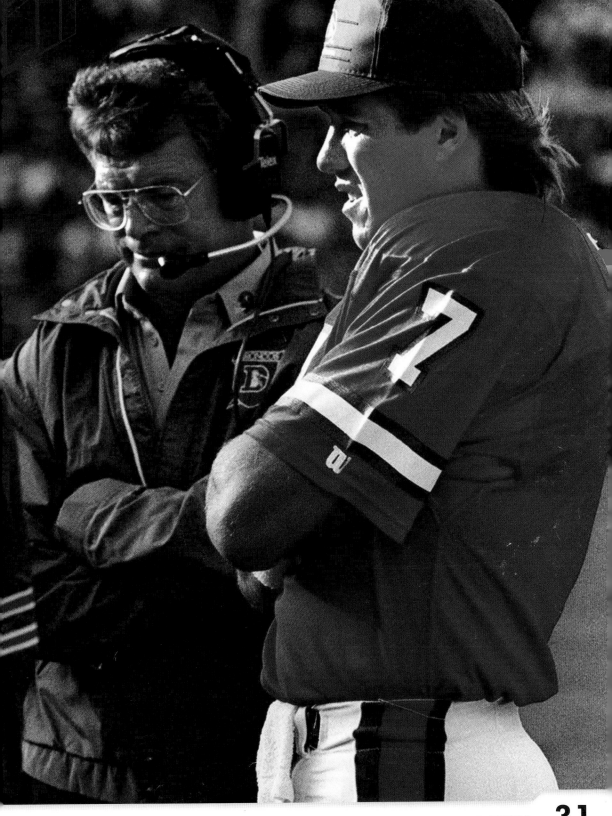

they had. They knew they could win with No. 7 under center.

"When the game is on the line, he has a different voice," once said Shannon Sharpe, a former Broncos tight end. "It gets slower, calmer. You know something magical will happen."

Elway's breakout moment came on January 11, 1987. It was his fourth season. He had guided the Broncos to the AFC Championship Game for the first time since 1977. Playing in Cleveland, the Broncos trailed the Browns 20–13 with 5:43 left. Denver got the ball on the 2-yard line, needing to go 98 yards for a game-tying touchdown. "We got 'em right where we want 'em," Broncos lineman Keith Bishop told his teammates.

Elway marched the Broncos all the way down the field, using 15 plays to cover the 98 yards.

He threw a 5-yard touchdown pass to Mark Jackson with 37 seconds left. Then came an extra point by Rich Karlis. The score was tied. Karlis booted a 33-yard field goal in overtime to give the Broncos a 23–20 win. That sent them to their second Super Bowl, which they lost to the New York Giants 39–20. The victory over the Browns that put the Broncos in Super Bowl XXI has been remembered for what has come to be known as "The Drive."

0-FOR-3

Although the Broncos played in three Super Bowls from the 1986 season to the 1989 season, they did not win any of them. In Super Bowl XXI in Pasadena, California, the Broncos lost to the New York Giants 39–20. In Super Bowl XXII in San Diego, California, the Broncos led 10–0 but lost to the Washington Redskins 42–10. John Elway's third chance at a win came in Super Bowl XXIV in New Orleans, Louisiana. The Broncos lost that one too, 55–10 against the San Francisco 49ers.

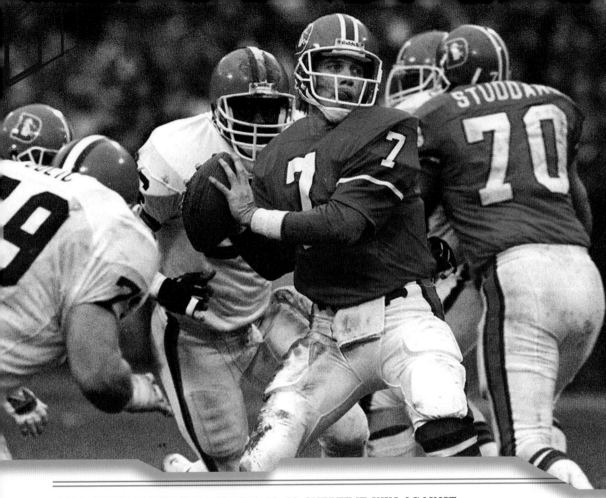

JOHN ELWAY PASSES IN DENVER'S 23–20 OVERTIME WIN AGAINST CLEVELAND IN THE AFC CHAMPIONSHIP GAME ON JANUARY 11, 1987.

The next season, the Broncos went back to the Super Bowl. Again they beat the Browns in the AFC title game, this time 38–33 in Denver. That game's famous play is known as "The Fumble." The Browns' Earnest Byner fumbled at the Broncos' goal line in the final minutes.

After the 1989 season, the Broncos and Browns again met in the AFC Championship Game. Again the Broncos came out on top. This one was not as close, however, with host Denver winning 37–21.

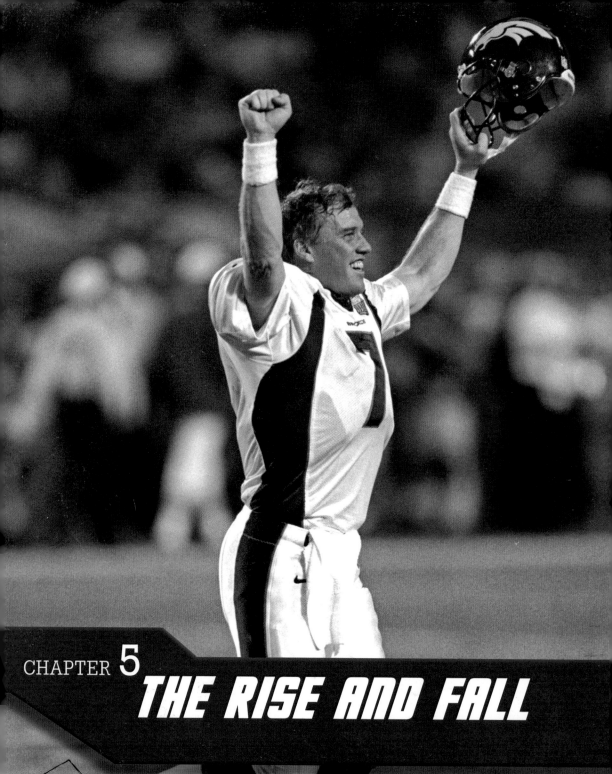

CHAPTER 5

THE RISE AND FALL

Despite a humbling 55–10 loss to the San Francisco 49ers in Super Bowl XXIV, the Broncos remained competitive. However, it would be a while before they would regain their elite status. Dan Reeves was fired after an 8–8 season in 1992. Although he won more games, 117, than any coach in team history at the time, the Broncos were once again in need of a change.

Wade Phillips replaced Reeves. But he lasted just two mediocre seasons before he was fired and succeeded by Mike Shanahan.

It took the Broncos a year to adjust to Shanahan's style. Then, in 1996, they tied for the best regular-season record in the NFL. They went 13–3 that season but suffered a surprising 30–27 loss to the expansion Jacksonville Jaguars in the second round of the playoffs. The Jaguars were playing in just their second season in the NFL.

JOHN ELWAY CELEBRATES THE BRONCOS' SECOND STRAIGHT SUPER BOWL WIN, 34–19 OVER THE FALCONS ON JANUARY 31, 1999.

"Without question, this is the toughest loss I've ever faced," tight end Shannon Sharpe said.

BUILDING A WINNER

Mike Shanahan was hired as the Broncos' coach in 1995. A former assistant coach with the Broncos, he was the San Francisco 49ers' offensive coordinator in 1994, helping them to a victory in Super Bowl XXIX. Shanahan brought that winning attitude to Denver and led the Broncos to their first two Super Bowl wins. Shanahan coached Denver for 14 years. His 146–91 record, including playoff games, was the best mark, through the 2009 season, for any Broncos coach.

That was the last time the Broncos would lose a playoff game with John Elway at quarterback. After a 12–4 season in 1997, they routed Jacksonville 42–17 in their playoff opener before winning 14–10 at Kansas City and 24–21 at Pittsburgh. Then they won it all.

With Elway, running back Terrell Davis, and a good defense leading the way, the Broncos defeated Green Bay 31–24 in Super Bowl XXXII. Elway finished 12-for-22 passing for 123 yards with one interception. He ran five times for 17 yards and a touchdown. "Other than my wife and four kids, there's nothing better than this. I can't believe it. I can't express it in words," Elway said.

Once the Broncos won a Super Bowl, they wanted another title. The 1998 season was even better than 1997. The Broncos started the season 13–0, went 14–2, and then cruised through the playoffs. They defeated the Miami Dolphins and New York Jets before taking care of the Atlanta Falcons 34–19 in Super Bowl XXXIII. Elway finished

DENVER'S TERRELL DAVIS RUNS PAST GREEN BAY'S BRIAN WILLIAMS IN SUPER BOWL XXXII. DAVIS WAS THE NFL'S MVP FOR THE 1998 SEASON.

18-for-29 passing for 336 yards and one touchdown with an interception. He also ran for a 3-yard touchdown.

The Broncos advanced to the playoffs 10 times and played in five Super Bowls during Elway's career. He announced his retirement a few months after the Super Bowl XXXIII victory.

Since Elway retired, the Broncos have not been as successful. The high point came in 2005, when Shanahan and quarterback Jake Plummer led the

REPLACING ELWAY

Since John Elway retired after the 1998 season, the Broncos have been on a quest to find someone to fill his shoes. Brian Griese, Jake Plummer, Jay Cutler, and Kyle Orton have taken their turns as the Broncos' starting quarterback. Although all four have had some success, none of them has been able to hold the job long.

team to a 13–3 record. Denver made the AFC title game but lost at home to Pittsburgh.

Reaching the Super Bowl in 1977 gave the Broncos a taste for success. Getting there five more times—and winning two championships—raised expectations in Denver. Shanahan expected the Broncos to compete for Super Bowl titles every year. But without Elway, they have come up short. That led to Shanahan being fired after the 2008 season.

Shanahan's replacement was 32-year-old Josh McDaniels. He brought with him a history of winning as an assistant coach with the New England Patriots. Like so many other coaches throughout Broncos history, McDaniels faces the challenge of rebuilding the Broncos into a

BRONCOS COACH JOSH MCDANIELS AND QUARTERBACK KYLE ORTON TALK DURING A GAME IN 2009. MCDANIELS SUCCEEDED MIKE SHANAHAN AS COACH.

winning team. McDaniels got off to a good start in his first season, leading the Broncos to a 6–0 record to begin 2009. The Broncos lost eight of their final 10 games, however, and did not qualify for the playoffs. Defensive end/linebacker Elvis Dumervil's season was a highlight for Denver. He led the NFL with 17 sacks.

John Ralston, Red Miller, Reeves, and Shanahan were all able to turn around the fortunes of the Broncos and provide the team, and the city of Denver, with remarkable memories. McDaniels hopes to add to the legacy.

DENVER'S ELVIS DUMERVIL SACKS PHILADELPHIA QUARTERBACK DONOVAN MCNABB. DUMERVIL LED THE NFL WITH 17 SACKS IN THE 2009 SEASON.

JOSH MCDANIELS

When the Broncos hired Josh McDaniels as coach in January 2009, he was the youngest person to hold that title in the NFL. He was just 32 years old.

McDaniels landed a job with the New England Patriots in 2001 as a personnel assistant and worked his way up to offensive coordinator in 2006. McDaniels was a staff member for all three of the Patriots' Super Bowl-winning teams in the 2000s.

Some football followers wondered, though, whether McDaniels's age would work against him as a head coach. He and talented Broncos quarterback Jay Cutler got into a dispute shortly after McDaniels was hired. Denver then traded Cutler to the Chicago Bears. Quarterback Kyle Orton was sent to the Broncos as part of the deal. Denver started 6–0 in 2009 but finished just 8–8. The jury was still out on whether McDaniels would be successful with the Broncos.

TIMELINE

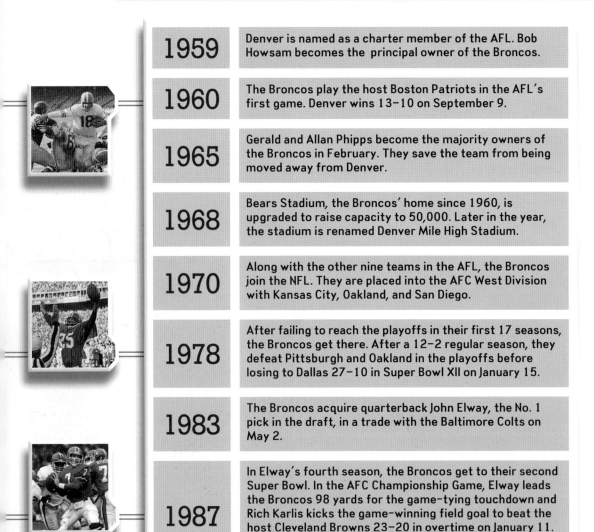

1959	Denver is named as a charter member of the AFL. Bob Howsam becomes the principal owner of the Broncos.
1960	The Broncos play the host Boston Patriots in the AFL's first game. Denver wins 13–10 on September 9.
1965	Gerald and Allan Phipps become the majority owners of the Broncos in February. They save the team from being moved away from Denver.
1968	Bears Stadium, the Broncos' home since 1960, is upgraded to raise capacity to 50,000. Later in the year, the stadium is renamed Denver Mile High Stadium.
1970	Along with the other nine teams in the AFL, the Broncos join the NFL. They are placed into the AFC West Division with Kansas City, Oakland, and San Diego.
1978	After failing to reach the playoffs in their first 17 seasons, the Broncos get there. After a 12–2 regular season, they defeat Pittsburgh and Oakland in the playoffs before losing to Dallas 27–10 in Super Bowl XII on January 15.
1983	The Broncos acquire quarterback John Elway, the No. 1 pick in the draft, in a trade with the Baltimore Colts on May 2.
1987	In Elway's fourth season, the Broncos get to their second Super Bowl. In the AFC Championship Game, Elway leads the Broncos 98 yards for the game-tying touchdown and Rich Karlis kicks the game-winning field goal to beat the host Cleveland Browns 23–20 in overtime on January 11. The Broncos go on to Super Bowl XXI, in which they lose to the New York Giants 39–20 on January 25.

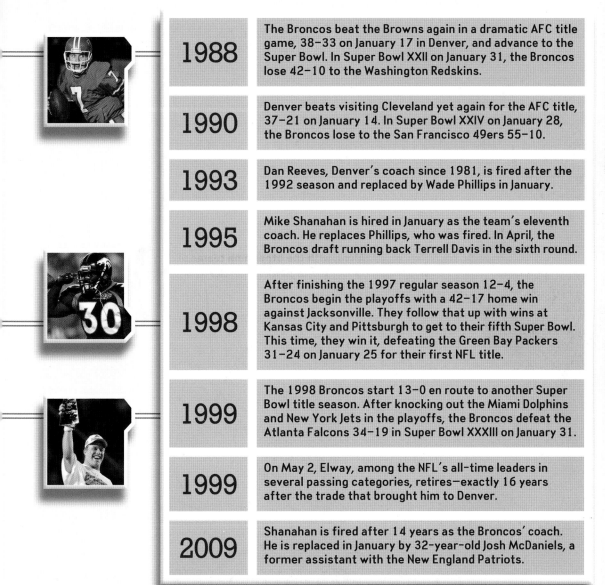

1988
The Broncos beat the Browns again in a dramatic AFC title game, 38–33 on January 17 in Denver, and advance to the Super Bowl. In Super Bowl XXII on January 31, the Broncos lose 42–10 to the Washington Redskins.

1990
Denver beats visiting Cleveland yet again for the AFC title, 37–21 on January 14. In Super Bowl XXIV on January 28, the Broncos lose to the San Francisco 49ers 55–10.

1993
Dan Reeves, Denver's coach since 1981, is fired after the 1992 season and replaced by Wade Phillips in January.

1995
Mike Shanahan is hired in January as the team's eleventh coach. He replaces Phillips, who was fired. In April, the Broncos draft running back Terrell Davis in the sixth round.

1998
After finishing the 1997 regular season 12–4, the Broncos begin the playoffs with a 42–17 home win against Jacksonville. They follow that up with wins at Kansas City and Pittsburgh to get to their fifth Super Bowl. This time, they win it, defeating the Green Bay Packers 31–24 on January 25 for their first NFL title.

1999
The 1998 Broncos start 13–0 en route to another Super Bowl title season. After knocking out the Miami Dolphins and New York Jets in the playoffs, the Broncos defeat the Atlanta Falcons 34–19 in Super Bowl XXXIII on January 31.

1999
On May 2, Elway, among the NFL's all-time leaders in several passing categories, retires—exactly 16 years after the trade that brought him to Denver.

2009
Shanahan is fired after 14 years as the Broncos' coach. He is replaced in January by 32-year-old Josh McDaniels, a former assistant with the New England Patriots.

QUICK STATS

FRANCHISE HISTORY

1960–

SUPER BOWLS
(wins in bold)

1977 (XII), 1986 (XXI), 1987 (XXII), 1989 (XXIV), **1997 (XXXII)**, **1998 (XXXIII)**

AFC CHAMPIONSHIP GAMES
(since 1970 AFL-NFL merger)

1977, 1986, 1987, 1989, 1991, 1997, 1998, 2005

DIVISION CHAMPIONSHIPS
(since 1970 AFL-NFL merger)

1977, 1978, 1984, 1986, 1987, 1989, 1991, 1996, 1998, 2005

KEY PLAYERS
(position, seasons with team)

Steve Atwater (S, 1989–98)
Terrell Davis (RB, 1995–2002)
John Elway (QB, 1983–98)
Randy Gradishar (LB, 1974–83)
Tom Jackson (LB, 1973–86)
Floyd Little (RB, 1967–75)
Karl Mecklenburg (LB, 1983–94)
Shannon Sharpe (TE; 1990–99, 2002–03)
Rod Smith (WR, 1995–2007)
Lionel Taylor (WR, 1960–66)
Louis Wright (CB, 1975–86)
Gary Zimmerman (OT, 1993–97)

KEY COACHES

Dan Reeves (1981–92):
110–73–1; 7–6 (playoffs)
Mike Shanahan (1995–2008):
138–86–0; 8–5 (playoffs)

HOME FIELDS

Invesco Field at Mile High (2001–)
Mile High Stadium (1960–2000) Known as Bears Stadium from 1960 to 1967

* All statistics through 2009 season

QUOTES AND ANECDOTES

In addition to playing for the Broncos, defensive end Lyle Alzado was a Cleveland Brown and an Oakland Raider. Throughout his 15-year career, he was known for his intimidating and tough play on the field. Off the field, he showed his soft side by helping sick children and doing other charity work. "It takes an awful lot of my time," he said. "But I need to help kids. I talk to kids every chance I have."

Wide receiver Rod Smith was not drafted when he came out of Missouri Southern State. Then he spent his first year, 1994, on the Broncos' practice squad and most of the next two seasons on the bench. Despite all that, Smith held team records for career receptions (849), career receiving yards (11,389), and career touchdown receptions (68) through 2009.

"You always knew you had a chance with him on the football field at the end of the game. You'd be excited just to see what he'd do this time. And you could see the looks of fear in the eyes of guys across the line."
—Mark Schlereth, ex-Broncos guard, on playing with quarterback John Elway

During the Broncos' run of Super Bowls in the 1980s, a trio of wide receivers rose to fame in Denver. Mark Jackson, Vance Johnson, and Ricky Nattiel were known as the "Three Amigos." None of them ever made a Pro Bowl. But they all had their great moments on the field. Jackson caught the game-tying touchdown during "The Drive" in Cleveland in January 1987. Johnson finished his career second on the Broncos' all-time receiving list. Nattiel caught several big touchdown passes, including one near the start of Super Bowl XXII. They are best known as a trio, however, and they played up their fame. There was even a song and video about them that included the line "Three Amigos, Touchdown Banditos!"

GLOSSARY

American Football League

A professional football league that operated from 1960 to 1969 before merging with the National Football League.

conclusion

The end or close.

consider

To think carefully about something in order to make a decision.

coexist

To come into being together.

debt

Something that is owed.

display

To show or make visible.

draft

A system used by professional sports leagues to select new players in order to spread incoming talent among all teams.

knack

A special skill or talent.

legacy

Anything handed down from the past.

mediocre

Neither good nor bad.

merge

To unite into a single body.

momentum

A continued strong performance based on recent success.

retire

To officially end one's career.

rookie

A first-year professional athlete.

stability

Continuing without change.

FOR MORE INFORMATION

Further Reading

Little, Floyd, and Tom Mackie. *Floyd Little's Tales from the Broncos Sideline.* Champaign, IL: Sports Publishing LLC, 2006.

Saccomano, Jim. *Denver Broncos: The Complete Illustrated History.* Minneapolis, MN: MBI Publishing Company, 2009.

Sports Illustrated. *The Football Book Expanded Edition.* New York: Sports Illustrated Books, 2009.

Web Links

To learn more about the Denver Broncos, visit ABDO Publishing Company online at **www.abdopublishing.com**. Web sites about the Broncos are featured on our Book Links page. These links are routinely monitored and updated to provide the most current information available.

Places to Visit

Denver Broncos Headquarters
13655 Broncos Parkway
Englewood, CO 80112
303-649-9000
The Broncos hold practice here, and during training camp the public can attend many of the practice sessions.

Invesco Field at Mile High
1701 Bryant Street
Denver, CO 80204
720-258-3000
www.invescofieldatmilehigh.com
This is the Broncos' home field. They play eight games here in the regular season.

Pro Football Hall of Fame
2121 George Halas Drive Northwest
Canton, OH 44708
330-456-8207
www.profootballhof.com
This hall of fame and museum highlights the greatest players and moments in the history of the National Football League. As of 2010, five players affiliated with the Broncos were enshrined, including John Elway and Floyd Little.

INDEX

About the Author

Brian Howell is a freelance writer based in Denver, Colorado. He has been a sports journalist for more than 17 years, writing about high school and college athletics, as well as covering major professional sporting events such as the U.S. Open golf tournament, the World Series, and the Stanley Cup playoffs. He has covered the Denver Broncos for the past three years for the *Longmont Times-Call*. He has earned several writing awards during his career. He lives with his wife and four children.